How Things Work

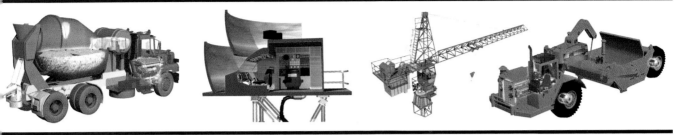

MONSTER MACHINES

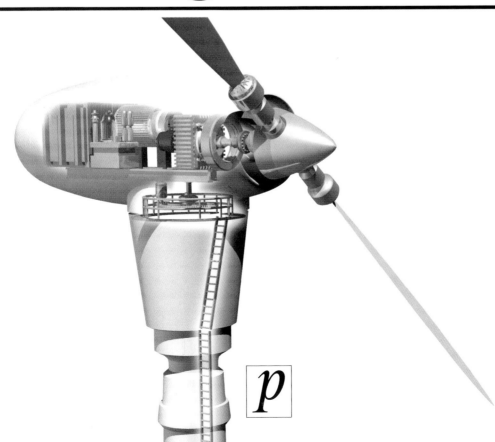

p

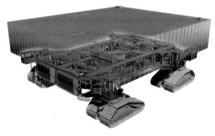

This is a Parragon Book
This edition published in 2001

Parragon
Queen Street House
4 Queen Street
Bath BA1 1HE, UK

ISBN 0-75255-295-3

Printed in Dubai, U.A.E

Produced by
Monkey Puzzle Media Ltd
Gissing's Farm
Fressingfield
Suffolk IP21 5SH
UK

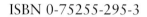

Illustrations: Alex Pang, Cara Kong,
Adrian Wright and Studio Liddell
Designer: Tim Mayer
Cover design: David West Children's Books
Editor: Linda Sonntag
Editorial assistance: Lynda Lines and Jenny Siklós
Indexer: Caroline Hamilton
Project manager: Katie Orchard

Photos supplied by MPM Images

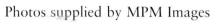

Contents

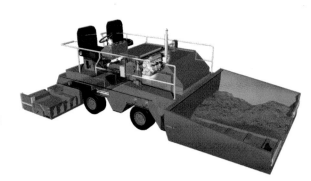

BUCKETWHEEL EXCAVATOR

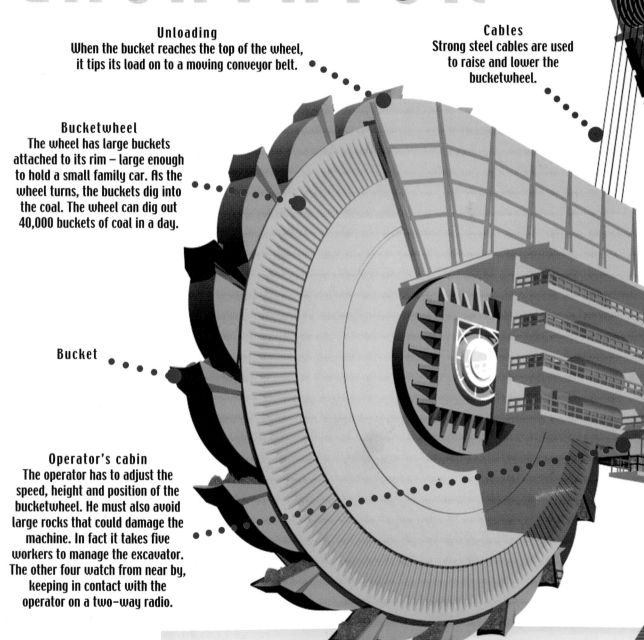

Unloading
When the bucket reaches the top of the wheel, it tips its load on to a moving conveyor belt.

Cables
Strong steel cables are used to raise and lower the bucketwheel.

Bucketwheel
The wheel has large buckets attached to its rim – large enough to hold a small family car. As the wheel turns, the buckets dig into the coal. The wheel can dig out 40,000 buckets of coal in a day.

Bucket

Operator's cabin
The operator has to adjust the speed, height and position of the bucketwheel. He must also avoid large rocks that could damage the machine. In fact it takes five workers to manage the excavator. The other four watch from near by, keeping in contact with the operator on a two-way radio.

Open-cast mine
A large mine, such as the open-cast copper mine at Bingham Canyon, near Salt Lake City, Utah, USA, can produce 270,000 tonnes (265,680 tons) of ore in a day. The deepest open-cast mine in the world is near Bergheim, Germany. It is 325 metres (1066 feet) deep.

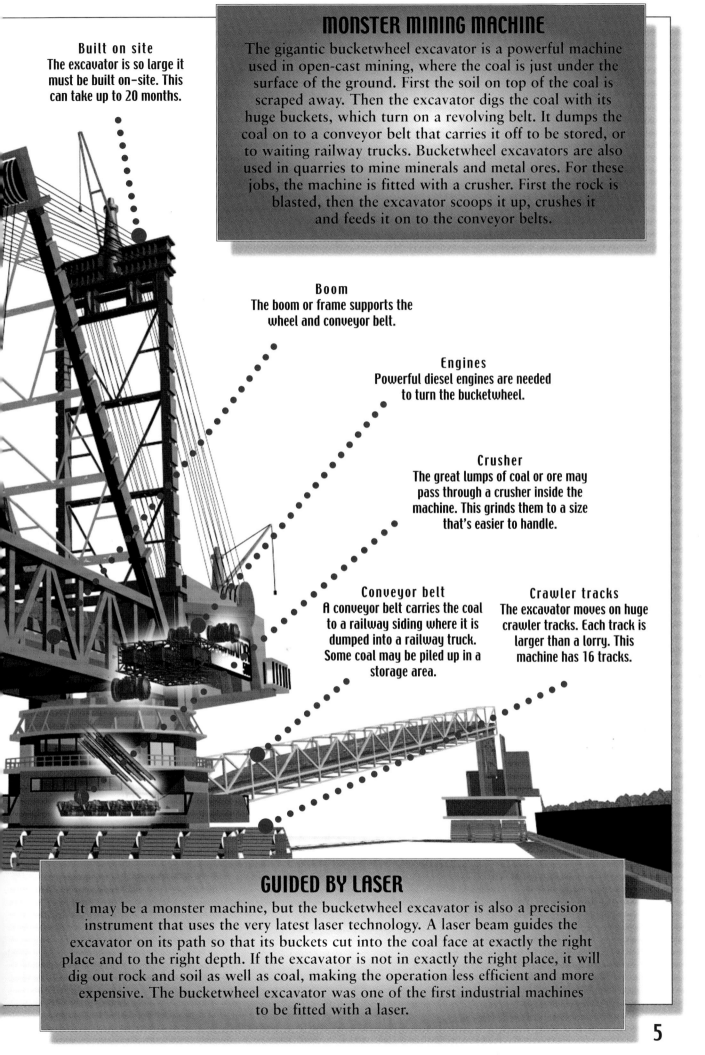

MONSTER MINING MACHINE

The gigantic bucketwheel excavator is a powerful machine used in open-cast mining, where the coal is just under the surface of the ground. First the soil on top of the coal is scraped away. Then the excavator digs the coal with its huge buckets, which turn on a revolving belt. It dumps the coal on to a conveyor belt that carries it off to be stored, or to waiting railway trucks. Bucketwheel excavators are also used in quarries to mine minerals and metal ores. For these jobs, the machine is fitted with a crusher. First the rock is blasted, then the excavator scoops it up, crushes it and feeds it on to the conveyor belts.

Built on site
The excavator is so large it must be built on-site. This can take up to 20 months.

Boom
The boom or frame supports the wheel and conveyor belt.

Engines
Powerful diesel engines are needed to turn the bucketwheel.

Crusher
The great lumps of coal or ore may pass through a crusher inside the machine. This grinds them to a size that's easier to handle.

Conveyor belt
A conveyor belt carries the coal to a railway siding where it is dumped into a railway truck. Some coal may be piled up in a storage area.

Crawler tracks
The excavator moves on huge crawler tracks. Each track is larger than a lorry. This machine has 16 tracks.

GUIDED BY LASER

It may be a monster machine, but the bucketwheel excavator is also a precision instrument that uses the very latest laser technology. A laser beam guides the excavator on its path so that its buckets cut into the coal face at exactly the right place and to the right depth. If the excavator is not in exactly the right place, it will dig out rock and soil as well as coal, making the operation less efficient and more expensive. The bucketwheel excavator was one of the first industrial machines to be fitted with a laser.

CONCRETE MIXER TRUCK

Drum
Just before the truck arrives at the building site, the driver pumps water into the drum. The drum turns about 12 times a minute to mix the concrete.

Hopper
Sand, cement dust and crushed rock are loaded into the drum through the hopper.

Mixing blades
Welded inside the drum are spiral-shaped blades called flights. These push the concrete to the front or back of the drum, depending on which way the drum is turning.

Unloading
To unload the concrete, the driver changes the direction of the drum. The concrete pours out of the drum on to the delivery chute.

Delivery chute
Concrete pours down the delivery chute to the concrete pump.

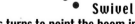

Delivery pipe
The concrete is pumped through a pipe on the outside of the boom. The pipe is made in sections that pass through the boom at the joints. This allows the pipe and boom to be folded for storage.

Swivel
This turns to point the boom in the correct direction so that the concrete goes where it is needed.

POURING CONCRETE
Concrete is pumped to the upper storeys of a tall building. The hopper delivering the concrete can move to allow the concrete to be spread wherever it is needed.

MIXING CONCRETE

Concrete is used to build tall blocks of offices and flats cheaply and quickly. It is a wet mixture of sand, cement, crushed rock and water that sets hard as it dries. When an office block is being built, wet concrete is poured into a steel framework, where it dries to form the floors and walls of the building. Concrete is made and delivered to the building site in a concrete mixer truck. The truck has a large revolving drum to hold the dry ingredients and the driver pumps in water just before the truck reaches the site. The drum turns all the time to keep the concrete well mixed and to stop it setting. The truck holds 15 tonnes (14.75 tons) of concrete. It is over 7 metres (24 feet) long and weighs 6 tonnes (just under 6 tons) when unloaded.

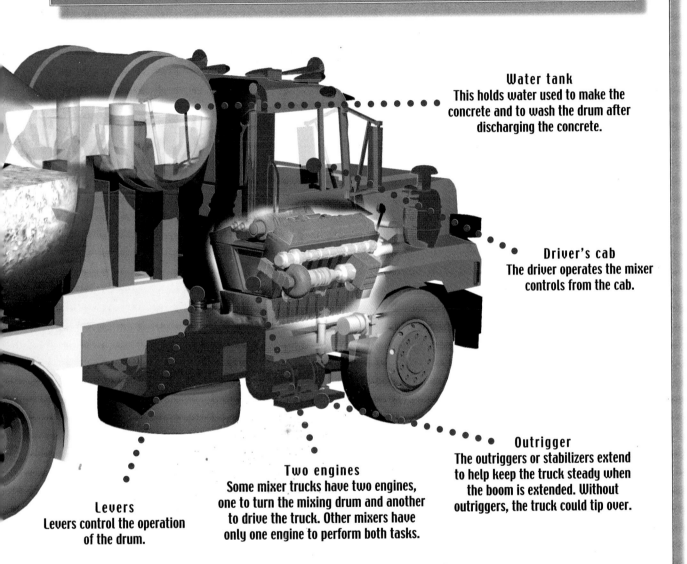

Water tank
This holds water used to make the concrete and to wash the drum after discharging the concrete.

Driver's cab
The driver operates the mixer controls from the cab.

Outrigger
The outriggers or stabilizers extend to help keep the truck steady when the boom is extended. Without outriggers, the truck could tip over.

Levers
Levers control the operation of the drum.

Two engines
Some mixer trucks have two engines, one to turn the mixing drum and another to drive the truck. Other mixers have only one engine to perform both tasks.

PUMPING CONCRETE

The mixer truck arrives at the building site and the driver unloads the concrete by reversing the direction of the mixing drum. The concrete flows down the delivery chute into a concrete pump. A piston in the pump forces the wet concrete through a long pipe and into the building. The machine has to be extremely powerful to pump concrete into the upper storeys. Workers smooth the concrete over the floor, or channel it into hollow casings to form the walls. When the concrete sets hard, the casing is removed.

EARTHSCRAPER

Steering mechanism
Hydraulic rams use the pressure of oil to generate the large force needed to turn the wheels.

Scraper control
This raises and lowers the cutting edge.

Quick-release mechanism
This releases the windows in an emergency.

Exhaust pipe
The fumes produced by the engine are carried away by the exhaust pipe.

Driver's cabin
An earthscraper is difficult to drive, as it has two separate engines to control. Also, the long body is articulated – it can bend in the middle.

Front engine
The front engine is a powerful four-stroke diesel engine with 16 cylinders, like a large truck engine.

Automatic gearbox
The gearbox automatically adjusts the amount of power fed to the wheels from the engine. Less power is needed in loose soils than in hard, compacted soils.

Powerful brakes
The earthscraper has powerful brakes. These work by pressing a pad called a brake shoe against a drum attached to each wheel.

SMOOTHING THE GROUND

An earthscraper is a huge machine used to level and smooth out large areas of ground. This machine is 15 metres (49 feet) long and 3.4 metres (11 feet) wide. It weighs 87 tonnes, (86 tons) as much as 60 family cars. Road-making teams use earthscrapers to cut through low hills so that a new road can be laid. The machine stores the soil it scrapes away. It can either dump it in one place to build up an embankment, or release it gradually, spreading it over the ground to fill small hollows.

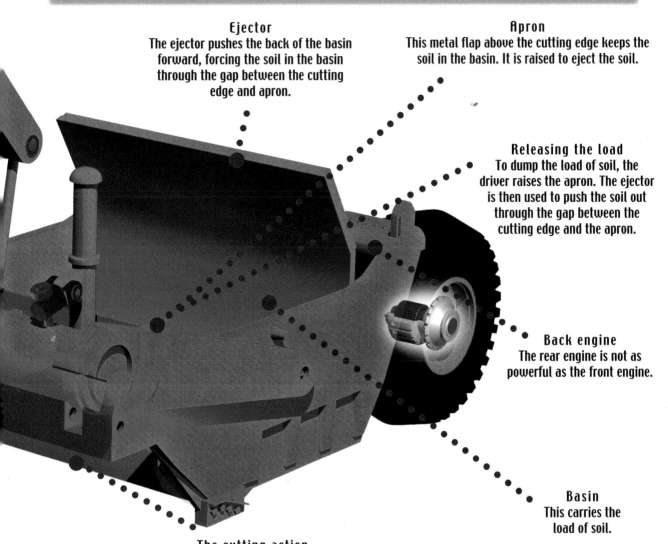

Ejector
The ejector pushes the back of the basin forward, forcing the soil in the basin through the gap between the cutting edge and apron.

Apron
This metal flap above the cutting edge keeps the soil in the basin. It is raised to eject the soil.

Releasing the load
To dump the load of soil, the driver raises the apron. The ejector is then used to push the soil out through the gap between the cutting edge and the apron.

Back engine
The rear engine is not as powerful as the front engine.

Basin
This carries the load of soil.

The cutting action
The cutting edge cuts 300 millimetres (12 inches) into the ground. It is lowered and the cutter slices easily through the ground – the soil curls up like butter on a knife. The soil moves into the basin where it is stored until dumping.

WORKING IN PAIRS

An earthscraper has two engines. One powers the front of the machine, where the driver sits, and the other powers the back, where the scraper cutting edge is. Often two earthscrapers are coupled together so a job can be done twice as fast. Double earthscrapers often bog down in soft ground. A bulldozer has to push them out. The back of the scraper is specially strengthened to cope with the force of the bulldozer.

POWER SHOVEL

Small shovel
This power shovel is a small one. It is only 13 metres (43 feet) long and weighs a mere 6 tonnes (just under 6 tons).

Boom

Open and shut
This ram uses oil pressure to transmit the force of a piston to the bucket bottom. This system, called a hydraulic ram, opens and closes the bucket.

Up and down
This hydraulic ram raises and lowers the boom.

Bucket
The bucket is hinged in the middle so it can open to drop a load. Some very big mining shovels have eight buckets fitted to a large wheel that revolves as the machine cuts into the coal-face.

Replaceable teeth
The teeth on the bucket are designed to sharpen themselves as they cut into the coal-face. They can be replaced when they eventually wear out.

Headlight
Powerful headlights shine on the coal-face for working at night.

Swing motor
The swing table is turned by an electric or hydraulic motor. This swings the boom round for unloading.

Bucket hinge
The bucket opens and shuts here.

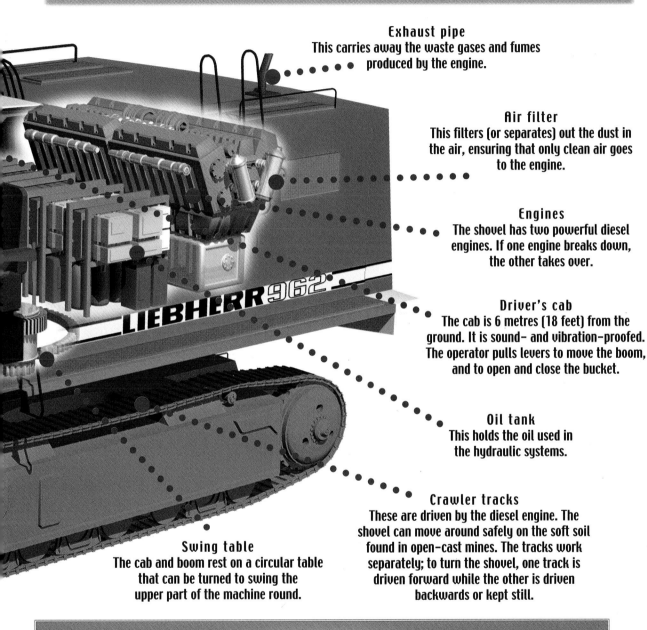

Exhaust pipe
This carries away the waste gases and fumes produced by the engine.

Air filter
This filters (or separates) out the dust in the air, ensuring that only clean air goes to the engine.

Engines
The shovel has two powerful diesel engines. If one engine breaks down, the other takes over.

Driver's cab
The cab is 6 metres (18 feet) from the ground. It is sound- and vibration-proofed. The operator pulls levers to move the boom, and to open and close the bucket.

Oil tank
This holds the oil used in the hydraulic systems.

Crawler tracks
These are driven by the diesel engine. The shovel can move around safely on the soft soil found in open-cast mines. The tracks work separately; to turn the shovel, one track is driven forward while the other is driven backwards or kept still.

Swing table
The cab and boom rest on a circular table that can be turned to swing the upper part of the machine round.

BIG DIGGER

A power shovel digs coal out of the walls of an open-cast coal mine. This monster machine has a huge bucket at the end of a long arm or boom – it carries up to 140 cubic metres (1,507 cubic feet) of coal. The boom stretches up the coal face to scrape out coal with the bucket. When the bucket is full, the driver swings the arm round and dumps the coal on to a waiting lorry. A power shovel works fast – it can fill a large lorry with 120 tonnes (118 tons) of coal in just two minutes. Power shovels are driven by petrol or diesel engines, or by electric motors.

The Marion 6360 power shovel has a boom length of 67 metres (220 feet) and a reach of 72 metres (236 feet). It weighs 1,100 tonnes (1,082 tons) and uses 20 electric motors to power the boom and bucket. It works in an open-cast coal mine near Percy in Illinois, USA.

TOWER CRANE

ANCHOR
The tower is anchored to large concrete blocks or set into a concrete base. Above 60 metres (200 feet), a tower crane is often linked to the building it is working on for extra stability.

Lifting winch
This winch winds in the hoist cables to lift the load. The rope is wound round a drum. The winch is powered by an electric motor.

Trolley winch
This winch winds in the cables attached to the trolley to move it along the main jib.

Counterweight jib
This long arm or jib carries the counterweights.

Driver's cab
The driver sits in a cab and controls the winches that move the trolley along the arm and lift the load. A worker on the ground guides the driver using a walkie-talkie radio. An alarm system in the cab warns the driver if a load is too heavy to lift.

Counterweights
These heavy concrete blocks balance the crane and stop it toppling over as it lifts a load.

Tower
The tower is made up of steel sections bolted together. Each section is 6 metres (20 feet) tall.

Ladder
The driver may have to climb over 100 steps to reach the cab.

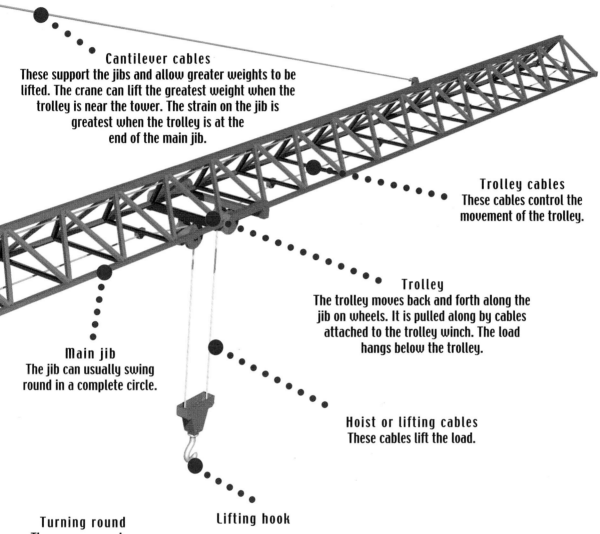

GOING UP

Tower cranes are built bit by bit on the building site. They get slowly taller as more sections are added to the tower. A small mobile crane places the first few sections of the tower in place. After that, a special section, called a climbing frame, is added. The crane lifts a new section and places it inside the climbing frame. A hydraulic ram, a lifting device at the base of the climbing frame, pushes the new section upwards. The climbing frame is then raised and the process repeated.

Cantilever cables
These support the jibs and allow greater weights to be lifted. The crane can lift the greatest weight when the trolley is near the tower. The strain on the jib is greatest when the trolley is at the end of the main jib.

Trolley cables
These cables control the movement of the trolley.

Trolley
The trolley moves back and forth along the jib on wheels. It is pulled along by cables attached to the trolley winch. The load hangs below the trolley.

Main jib
The jib can usually swing round in a complete circle.

Hoist or lifting cables
These cables lift the load.

Turning round
The crane can swing round in a complete circle on a revolving plate. The plate is turned by an electric motor.

Lifting hook

BUILDING SKYSCRAPERS

Tower cranes are the tallest cranes in the world. They are used to help build tall buildings such as skyscrapers. They lift things to the top of the building under construction. A tower crane has a long horizontal arm, called a jib, which turns on top of a tall tower. The jib carries a movable trolley, from which the load hangs on steel cables. Electric motors connected to winches wind in the cables attached to the load and trolley. The cables pass around pulleys, which reduce the force needed to lift the load. However, using pulleys increases the length of cable that has to be wound in.

PAPER-MAKING MACHINE

SPECIAL PAPER
Small paper-making machines are used to make special or high-quality paper. This is used in expensive books and presentation scrolls.

Support mesh
Wire mesh supports the wet layer of pulp while the water drains and is sucked out. The web is then strong enough to be lifted off the mesh of wire.

Keeping watch
Workers can walk around the walkway at the top of the machine to keep watch and make repairs.

Felt belt
The felt belt carries the wet web to the press rollers.

Pulp mixture
It takes 12 trees to make 1 tonne (about 1 ton) of paper.

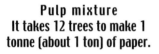

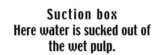

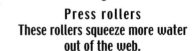

Suction box
Here water is sucked out of the wet pulp.

Press rollers
These rollers squeeze more water out of the web.

CHINESE PAPER
The Chinese discovered how to make paper about 2,000 years ago. They boiled old fish nets and rags with water, and then beat them to make a soft, wet pulp. A mesh made of fine criss-crossed wires was dipped into the pulp and then removed with a layer of pulp on it. After the water had drained away, the layer of pulp was pressed and dried to make paper.

TREES TO PULP

Today, paper-making is basically the same as it was 2,000 years ago, except that the raw material is wood from trees such as pine and spruce. They are grown in plantations specially for the paper industry. The paper-making machine was invented in 1803 by two English brothers, Henry and Sealy Fourdrinier. Paper-making machines are sometimes called Fourdrinier machines. First the wood is stripped of bark, then ground to a pulp by giant grinders. The pulp is cooked with chemicals to break it into fibres. Then it is washed, bleached and beaten to produce smaller, finer fibres. Finally, it is mixed with water and fed into the paper-making machine.

Calender rollers
The calender rollers smooth the surface of the paper.

Long machine
Paper-making machines are over 200 metres (650 feet) long and can produce more than 300 tonnes (295 tons) of paper in a day. Over 1,000 metres (3,280 feet) of paper races through the machine every minute.

Heated drying rollers
The heated drying rollers take water out of the paper in the form of steam.

Jumbo
The paper is wound on a large reel called a jumbo. It can be fitted and removed without stopping the machine.

Computer control panels
A computer checks the strength, thickness and colour of the paper. Only a few people are needed to look after the huge machine.

MAKING PAPER

In a paper-making machine, the wet pulp is spread on a wire mesh that turns on rollers. The mesh vibrates and the water drains out of the pulp, leaving a smooth layer of fibres, called the web. The web passes on to a moving belt made of felt. Then it goes through a series of rollers called press rollers, which squeeze out more water. The web next passes between heated drying cylinders, which remove the remaining water. Finally, the web passes through an upright stack of rollers, called the calender, which smooth its surface.

PRINTING PRESS

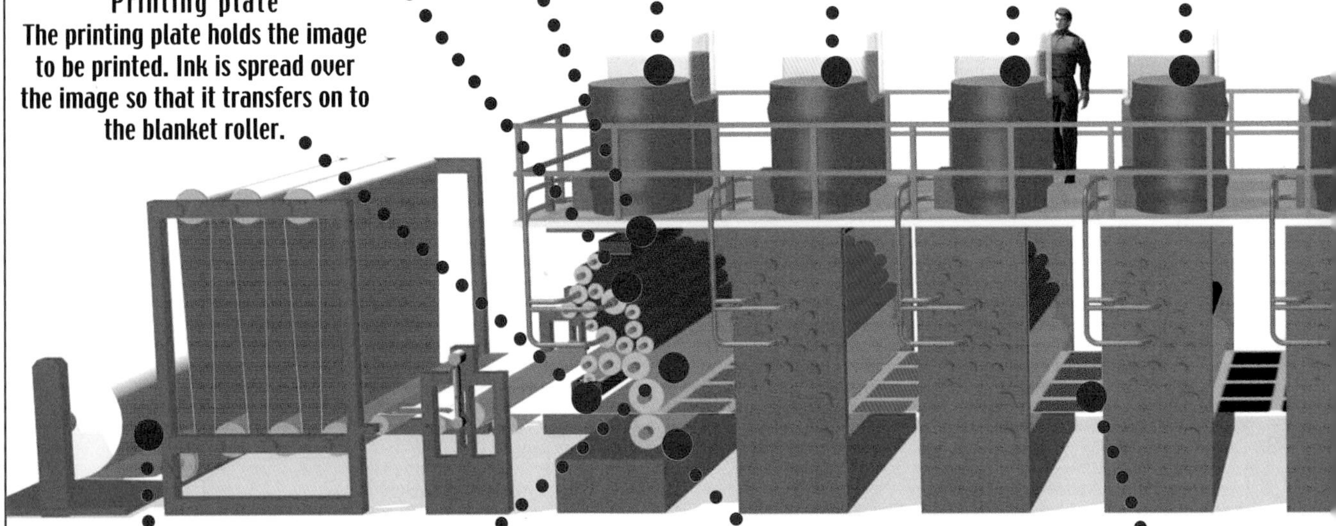

Inking rollers
There are different kinds of inking roller. Some have a rubber surface, others have a metal surface. They ensure that ink is spread evenly over the plate.

Ink trough
Each of the four presses has a trough that holds the ink.

Printing press 2 prints magenta (red).

Printing press 4 prints black.

Printing press 1 prints cyan (blue).

Printing press 3 prints yellow.

Printing plate
The printing plate holds the image to be printed. Ink is spread over the image so that it transfers on to the blanket roller.

Reel of paper
In an automated press, the reel can be changed without stopping the press.

Blanket roller
The rubber-coated blanket roller transfers the image from the plate to the paper. Its rubber surface prints evenly on the bumpy paper surface.

Transfer roller
The transfer roller carries the paper to the next printing plate. Mechanical grippers on the transfer drum hold the paper accurately in place so that the four colours are printed in register (in the correct place).

Paper web
The web, a continuous strip of paper, is fed through the press.

LETTERPRESS
Johann Gutenberg, a German goldsmith, invented printing using movable type in 1439. Individual letters were carved into small wooden blocks – the type. The blocks were placed in a frame, wiped with ink, and pressed on to paper to produce the printed page. This process is called letterpress printing. It is still used today, although offset lithography, shown here, is now much more common.

LITHOGRAPHY

In lithography, a thin metal sheet called a plate or stereo is used to print pages. An image of the text and pictures to be printed is formed photographically on the plate. The plate is treated with chemicals to make ink stick to the dark parts of the image. The plate is often wrapped around a cylinder which rotates at high speed. As the cylinder rotates, the plate is pressed against paper coming off a large reel. The ink transfers to the paper, forming the printed image. In a similar process called offset lithography, the image is first transferred to a rubber cylinder, called the blanket roller, which then prints on to paper.

PRINTING SHEETS

Small printing presses print sheets of paper. Sheet-fed machines are used for printing books which require good-quality printing, rather than many magazines and newspapers which are not intended to be kept for long.

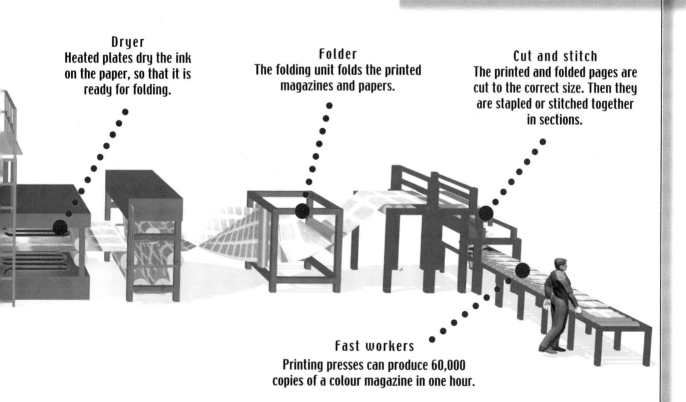

Dryer
Heated plates dry the ink on the paper, so that it is ready for folding.

Folder
The folding unit folds the printed magazines and papers.

Cut and stitch
The printed and folded pages are cut to the correct size. Then they are stapled or stitched together in sections.

Fast workers
Printing presses can produce 60,000 copies of a colour magazine in one hour.

PRINTING A PICTURE

Printed pictures are produced using a pattern of small dots of ink. There are many dots where the picture is dark and fewer where the picture is light. This allows the light and dark shades of the picture to be reproduced. To print a full-colour picture, four separate plates are made. One plate prints the cyan (blue) parts of the picture. Other plates print the magenta (red), yellow and black parts. All the colours in a picture can be reproduced using only these four colours.

17

THE LONDON EYE

Inside an egg
The 32 fully enclosed egg-shaped passenger cars or capsules, each weighing 9 tonnes (about 9 tons), and holding 25 people. The capsules are attached to the outer rim and each has an individual motor to rotate it as the wheel goes round. They are heated in winter and air-conditioned in summer.

Round and round
One circuit of the wheel takes half an hour.

By the river
The London Eye is located on the south bank of the River Thames. Although built to last 50 years, the wheel has planning permission for only five years. After that, Londoners will have to decide whether or not they want to keep it.

MONSTER TOURIST ATTRACTION
The London Eye was built as a tourist attraction to bring people to London for the year-2000 celebrations. The 1,500-tonne (1,475-ton) structure is heavier than 250 double-decker buses.

At night, the London Eye pulses gently with soft light, at 16 pulses a minute, our natural rate of breathing.

Foundations
The London Eye is built on 45 concrete piles sunk 33 metres (108 feet) deep, containing 2,600 tonnes (2,560 tons) of concrete.

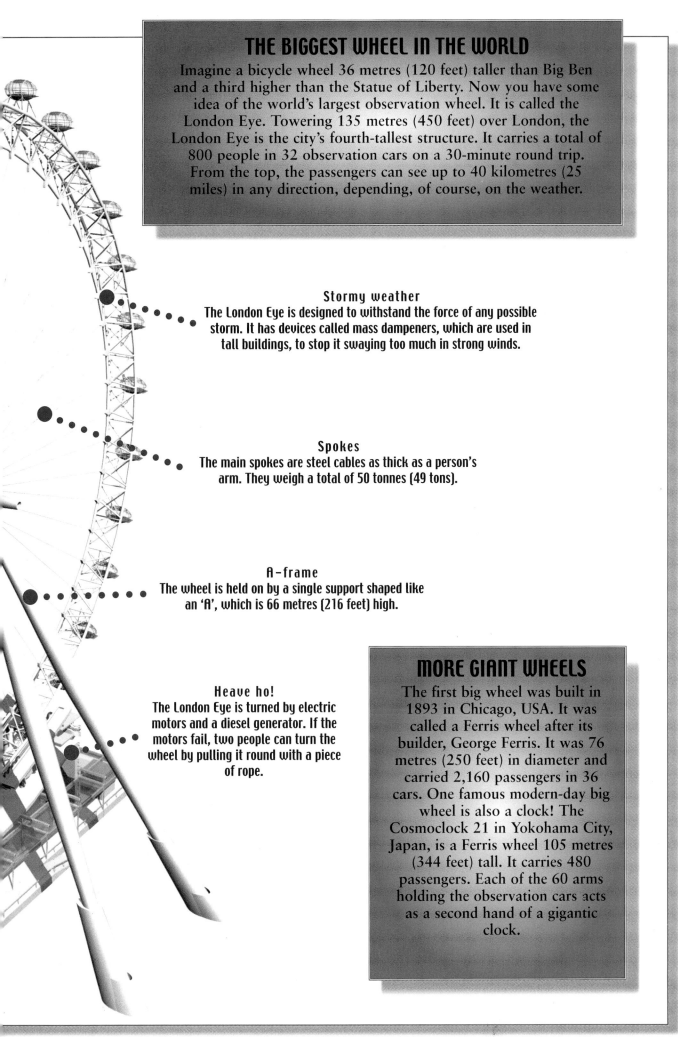

THE BIGGEST WHEEL IN THE WORLD

Imagine a bicycle wheel 36 metres (120 feet) taller than Big Ben and a third higher than the Statue of Liberty. Now you have some idea of the world's largest observation wheel. It is called the London Eye. Towering 135 metres (450 feet) over London, the London Eye is the city's fourth-tallest structure. It carries a total of 800 people in 32 observation cars on a 30-minute round trip. From the top, the passengers can see up to 40 kilometres (25 miles) in any direction, depending, of course, on the weather.

Stormy weather
The London Eye is designed to withstand the force of any possible storm. It has devices called mass dampeners, which are used in tall buildings, to stop it swaying too much in strong winds.

Spokes
The main spokes are steel cables as thick as a person's arm. They weigh a total of 50 tonnes (49 tons).

A-frame
The wheel is held on by a single support shaped like an 'A', which is 66 metres (216 feet) high.

Heave ho!
The London Eye is turned by electric motors and a diesel generator. If the motors fail, two people can turn the wheel by pulling it round with a piece of rope.

MORE GIANT WHEELS

The first big wheel was built in 1893 in Chicago, USA. It was called a Ferris wheel after its builder, George Ferris. It was 76 metres (250 feet) in diameter and carried 2,160 passengers in 36 cars. One famous modern-day big wheel is also a clock! The Cosmoclock 21 in Yokohama City, Japan, is a Ferris wheel 105 metres (344 feet) tall. It carries 480 passengers. Each of the 60 arms holding the observation cars acts as a second hand of a gigantic clock.

19

FLIGHT SIMULATOR

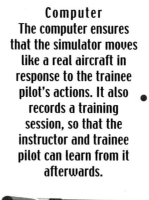

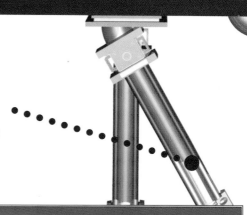

Instructor's console

Computer
The computer ensures that the simulator moves like a real aircraft in response to the trainee pilot's actions. It also records a training session, so that the instructor and trainee pilot can learn from it afterwards.

Instructor's console
The instructor sits at a console behind the trainee pilot. The console displays information about the pilot's performance. The instructor can tell the computer to simulate special conditions, such as foggy weather, or to give the trainee a difficult task, such as an emergency landing.

Pistons
The pistons tilt and roll the simulator to follow the pilot's commands. If the pilot pulls up on the joystick, the simulator tilts up to show that the aeroplane would tilt upwards. The pistons can also create the effect of air turbulence by making the simulator vibrate up and down.

LEARNING TO FLY

Trainee pilots can learn to fly an aeroplane without leaving the ground. They are trained on a computer-controlled machine called a flight simulator. This is a copy of a real cabin in which the trainee pilot sits. The simulator has all the control levers and instruments found in a real aeroplane cockpit, and the pilot 'flies' the simulator exactly as if it were the real thing. The computer makes the simulator react like an aeroplane: it tilts and rolls as the pilot moves the controls, and the instruments give realistic readings of such things as height and the amount of fuel left in the tanks. The simulator even reproduces the engine noise and the sound of air flowing past the aeroplane.

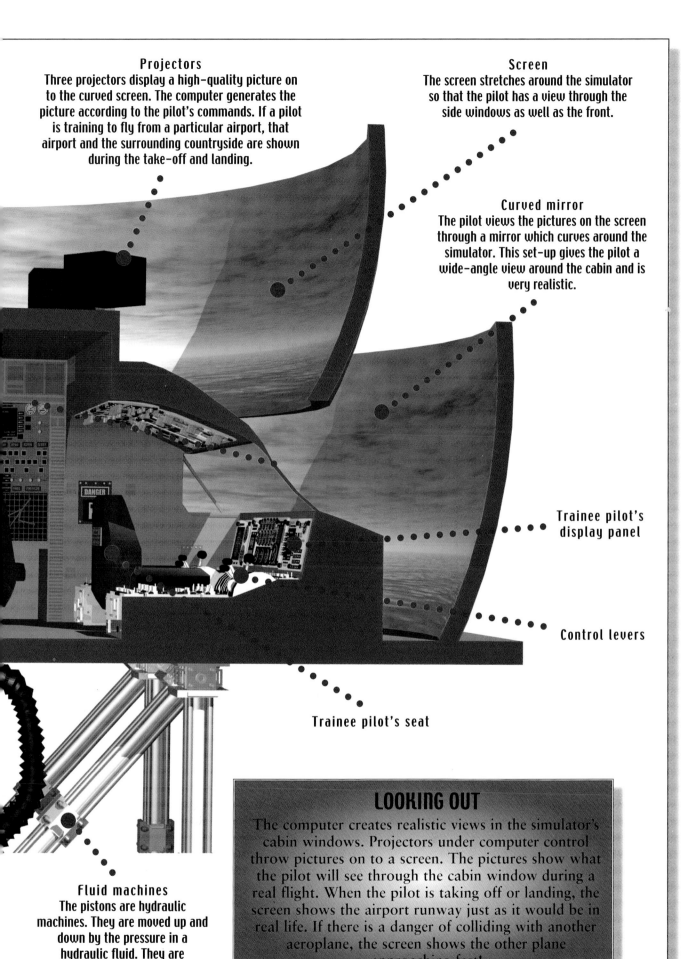

Projectors
Three projectors display a high-quality picture on to the curved screen. The computer generates the picture according to the pilot's commands. If a pilot is training to fly from a particular airport, that airport and the surrounding countryside are shown during the take-off and landing.

Screen
The screen stretches around the simulator so that the pilot has a view through the side windows as well as the front.

Curved mirror
The pilot views the pictures on the screen through a mirror which curves around the simulator. This set-up gives the pilot a wide-angle view around the cabin and is very realistic.

Trainee pilot's display panel

Control levers

Trainee pilot's seat

Fluid machines
The pistons are hydraulic machines. They are moved up and down by the pressure in a hydraulic fluid. They are controlled by the main computer and respond to the trainee pilot's actions.

LOOKING OUT
The computer creates realistic views in the simulator's cabin windows. Projectors under computer control throw pictures on to a screen. The pictures show what the pilot will see through the cabin window during a real flight. When the pilot is taking off or landing, the screen shows the airport runway just as it would be in real life. If there is a danger of colliding with another aeroplane, the screen shows the other plane approaching fast!

ROLLER-COASTER

Gravity
Most roller-coasters are powered by gravity. The cars are pulled to the top of a steep slope and let go. Gravity pulls them down the slope, gathering enough speed to climb the next hill.

Gaining weight
As the car moves up a slope or twist, you appear to gain weight because inertia presses you into the seat. Inertia is the tendency of things to stay still unless they are forced to move.

Losing weight
As the car moves down a slope, you appear to lose weight.

Power cables
Some roller-coasters are powered by electricity. There is an electric cable between the two rails.

MOMENTUM
When a roller-coaster suddenly dives down, your stomach seems to get 'left behind'. This happens because anything moving tends to keep going in one direction. This tendency is called momentum. If you were not strapped into your seat, momentum would continue to carry you uphill, and you would be thrown into the air as the car hurtled down.

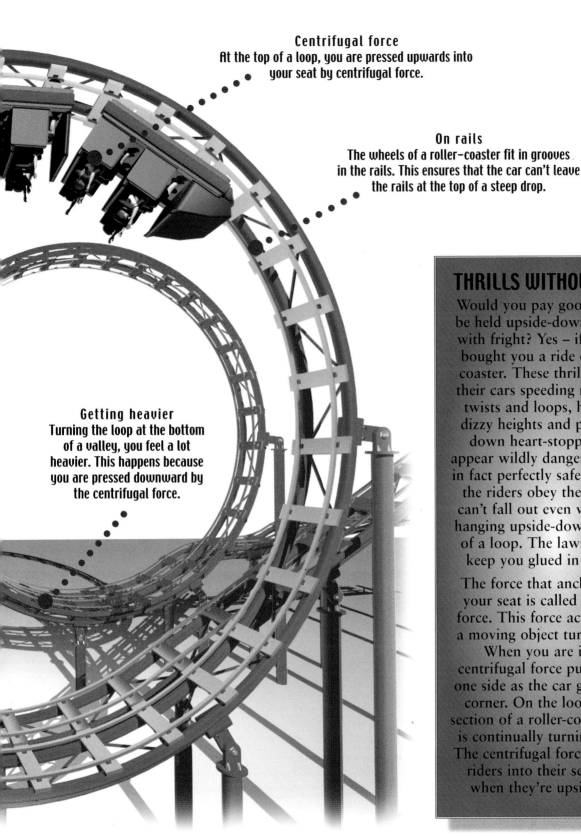

Centrifugal force
At the top of a loop, you are pressed upwards into your seat by centrifugal force.

On rails
The wheels of a roller-coaster fit in grooves in the rails. This ensures that the car can't leave the rails at the top of a steep drop.

Getting heavier
Turning the loop at the bottom of a valley, you feel a lot heavier. This happens because you are pressed downward by the centrifugal force.

THRILLS WITHOUT SPILLS

Would you pay good money to be held upside-down screaming with fright? Yes – if the money bought you a ride on a roller-coaster. These thrill rides with their cars speeding round crazy twists and loops, hurtling up dizzy heights and plummeting down heart-stopping drops appear wildly dangerous, but are in fact perfectly safe – as long as the riders obey the rules. You can't fall out even when you're hanging upside-down at the top of a loop. The laws of science keep you glued in your seat.

The force that anchors you in your seat is called centrifugal force. This force acts whenever a moving object turns a corner. When you are in a car, centrifugal force pushes you to one side as the car goes round a corner. On the loop-the-loop section of a roller-coaster, the car is continually turning a corner. The centrifugal force presses the riders into their seats – even when they're upside-down!

HIGHEST, FASTEST, LONGEST

The highest and fastest roller-coaster in the world is called *Superman – The Escape*. It is at Six Flags Magic Mountain, Valencia, California, USA. The cars reach a speed of 161 kph (100 mph). The structure is 126 metres (1,650 feet) tall. The longest roller-coaster in the world is at Lightwater Valley Theme Park in Ripon, Yorkshire, UK. Called *The Ultimate*, the ride is 2.29 kilometres (1 mile 740 yards) long.

23

OIL PLATFORM

PLUMBING THE DEPTHS

The world consumes over 68 million barrels of oil a day. Much of it comes from large oil rigs or platforms scattered across the oceans of the world. These platforms either float on the sea or stand on the sea-bed. They drill into the sea-bed to the oil deposits beneath it. The oil is pumped to the surface and carried by tanker or pipeline to refineries on land. Natural gas is often found with the oil and can be extracted at the same time.

Gas purification system
The natural gas that comes to the surface with the crude oil is a mixture of gases. The useful part of the mixture is separated out, turned to a liquid and sent ashore.

BRANCHING OUT

A system called directional drilling allows wells to be drilled at different angles rather than straight down. This means that many oilfields can be reached from one platform. A single platform can receive oil from up to 60 wells.

Platform support legs
The legs house the drill that digs its way down to the oilfield. Once a well has been drilled, the legs contain the pipes carrying oil, gas and water. The oil and gas are separated and purified. The gas is pumped to the mainland through pipes. When the pipeline is shut down, the gas is burnt, or flared off.

TYPES OF PLATFORM

A floating platform, or semi-submersible platform, rests on huge floats called pontoons. It is held in place above the oil well by steel cables that anchor each corner of the platform to the sea-bed. Some platforms, called guyed tower platforms, stand on a steel framework that reaches down to the sea-bed. The tower is anchored to the sea-bed with steel cables. Gravity platforms are the biggest and heaviest. These huge concrete structures rest directly on the sea-bed, held in place by their sheer weight. A platform is like a small town. It has its own power supply, water supply, living quarters, helicopter pad and medical facilities. Oil workers may live and work on the platforms for weeks at a time.

The tallest oil platform is the *Mars* platform in the Gulf of Mexico. It rises 896 metres (2,940 feet) from the ocean-bed to the surface of the sea. It stands twice as high as the Empire State Building. The *Mars* platform produces 38,000 barrels of oil per day.

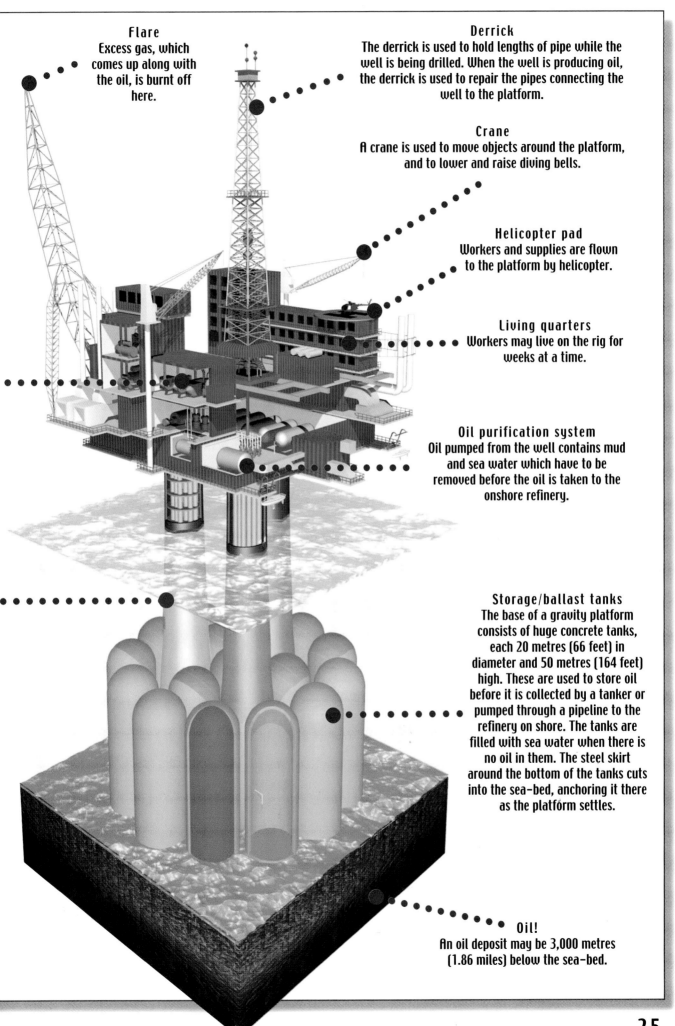

Flare
Excess gas, which comes up along with the oil, is burnt off here.

Derrick
The derrick is used to hold lengths of pipe while the well is being drilled. When the well is producing oil, the derrick is used to repair the pipes connecting the well to the platform.

Crane
A crane is used to move objects around the platform, and to lower and raise diving bells.

Helicopter pad
Workers and supplies are flown to the platform by helicopter.

Living quarters
Workers may live on the rig for weeks at a time.

Oil purification system
Oil pumped from the well contains mud and sea water which have to be removed before the oil is taken to the onshore refinery.

Storage/ballast tanks
The base of a gravity platform consists of huge concrete tanks, each 20 metres (66 feet) in diameter and 50 metres (164 feet) high. These are used to store oil before it is collected by a tanker or pumped through a pipeline to the refinery on shore. The tanks are filled with sea water when there is no oil in them. The steel skirt around the bottom of the tanks cuts into the sea-bed, anchoring it there as the platform settles.

Oil!
An oil deposit may be 3,000 metres (1.86 miles) below the sea-bed.

25

WIND TURBINE

WIND FARMS

A wind farm is a collection of wind turbines built on a high ridge, sea coast or open plain. There may be hundreds of wind turbines in a wind farm. The largest wind farms generate as much electricity as three power stations. There are around 20,000 wind turbines producing electricity in the world today.

Gearbox
A gearbox links the turbine blades to the electricity generator. The gearbox ensures that the generator turns at a high speed whatever the wind speed. When the wind is weak and turns the turbine blades slowly, the gearbox increases the speed of the generator.

Control system
The control system automatically adjusts the direction and angle of the blades. This is important as the maximum amount of power must be extracted from the wind.

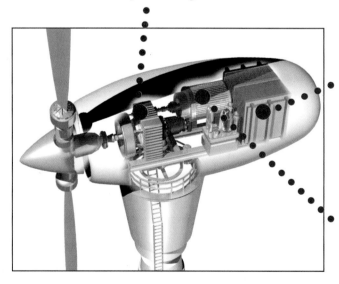

Generator
The generator produces electricity. Inside the generator a coil of wire turns near a magnet. An electric current is produced in the coil.

Cables
Underground cables carry the electricity to where it is needed.

POWER FROM THE WIND

For over 5,000 years, the wind has been used as a source of power. Windmills grind corn. Modern versions of the windmill generate electricity. These wind turbines, as they are called, have huge blades to catch the slightest wind. The blades are connected to an electricity generator. When the blades are turned by the wind, this turns the generator and produces electricity.

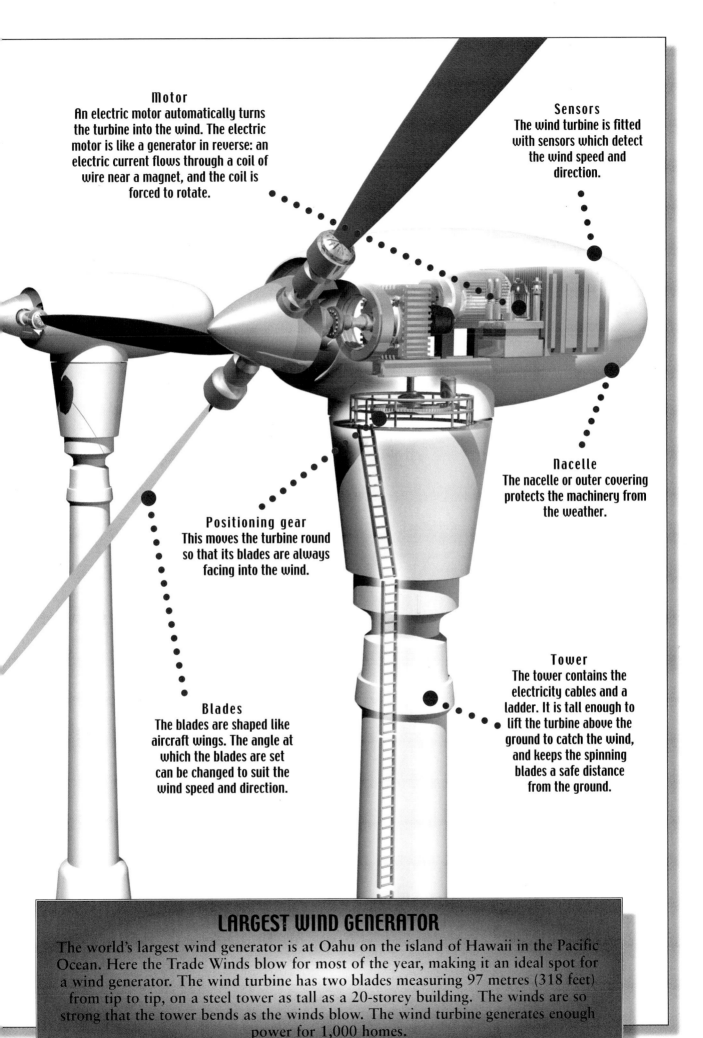

Motor
An electric motor automatically turns the turbine into the wind. The electric motor is like a generator in reverse: an electric current flows through a coil of wire near a magnet, and the coil is forced to rotate.

Sensors
The wind turbine is fitted with sensors which detect the wind speed and direction.

Nacelle
The nacelle or outer covering protects the machinery from the weather.

Positioning gear
This moves the turbine round so that its blades are always facing into the wind.

Tower
The tower contains the electricity cables and a ladder. It is tall enough to lift the turbine above the ground to catch the wind, and keeps the spinning blades a safe distance from the ground.

Blades
The blades are shaped like aircraft wings. The angle at which the blades are set can be changed to suit the wind speed and direction.

LARGEST WIND GENERATOR

The world's largest wind generator is at Oahu on the island of Hawaii in the Pacific Ocean. Here the Trade Winds blow for most of the year, making it an ideal spot for a wind generator. The wind turbine has two blades measuring 97 metres (318 feet) from tip to tip, on a steel tower as tall as a 20-storey building. The winds are so strong that the tower bends as the winds blow. The wind turbine generates enough power for 1,000 homes.

INDUSTRIAL ROBOT

Sensor
Robot arms contain sensors that detect where the arm is and feed this information to the computer control unit. The computer checks that the arm is in the correct position. If not, the computer activates the motors to move the arm.

Computer unit
The computer holds the program that guides the robot arm. It receives information from the arm sensors and controls the motors that move the arm.

Robot hand
Car assembly robots can be fitted with many different kinds of tool: welding units, nozzles for spraying paint, sanding discs for smoothing surfaces and electromagnets for lifting metal parts.

CAR-BUILDING ROBOTS

Most of the world's robots are employed in making cars. Each robot performs a single task on the car chassis as it moves along the production line.

TIRELESS WORKERS

The popular idea of a robot is a machine that looks and acts like a human. But most robots are industrial robots, and don't look like us at all. The industrial robot is a computer-controlled mechanical arm. Robot arms can bend in every direction. At the end of the arm is the robot 'hand'. This is a tool such as a welder, paint spray or gripper for grasping objects. These robots work round the clock in factories, doing jobs like welding metal parts together and painting the finished products. They live up to their name, since the word 'robot' comes from the Czech word for a slave.

ROBOT EYES

Some robots are fitted with vision units, or 'eyes', to increase their usefulness. A welding robot without vision must have the parts it is welding placed in exactly the right position. But a robot with vision can check the position of the parts and adjust its actions accordingly.

Welding metal
Welding is a process that joins pieces of metal together. The edges of the metal pieces are melted so that they flow together. Welding robots use a strong electric current to melt the metals.

Robot arm
The arm has shoulder, elbow and wrist joints that can move in any direction.

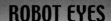

Power unit
A robot arm is moved by electric motors, or by liquid pressure (hydraulics). Electric motors are used in the joints that rotate. Hydraulic power is used in joints that move up and down.

TEACHING A ROBOT

An industrial robot has to be programmed like a computer, to tell it what to do. There are two main ways of instructing industrial robots. The first is to work out exactly what movements are needed to complete a task, and to write these movements into a program for the control computer. The second is to teach the robot a job such as painting, by guiding its arm through the movements needed to complete the task. The robot is programmed to remember what it has been taught, and will repeat the movements exactly.

SPACE STATION

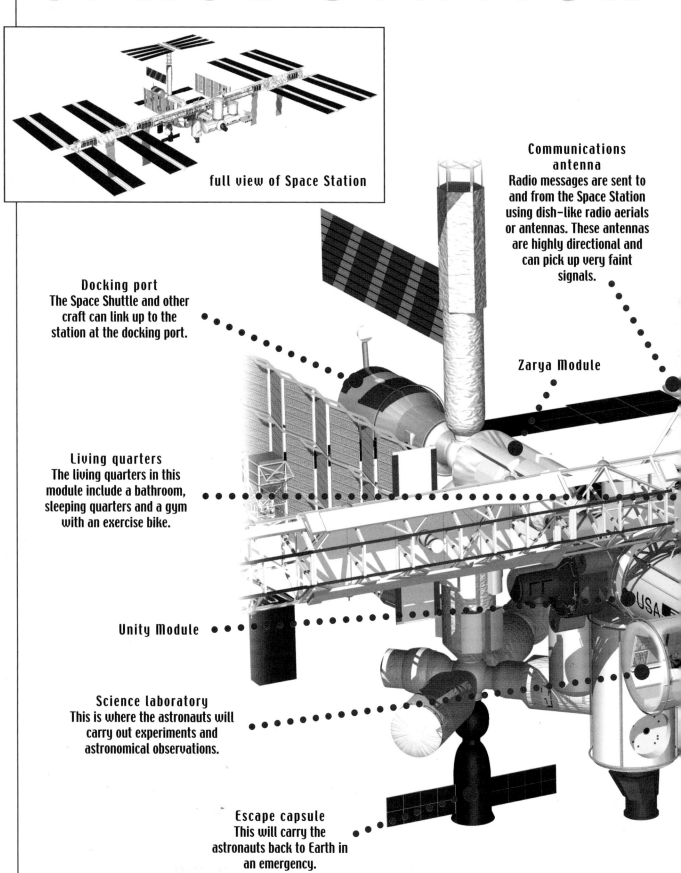

full view of Space Station

Docking port
The Space Shuttle and other craft can link up to the station at the docking port.

Living quarters
The living quarters in this module include a bathroom, sleeping quarters and a gym with an exercise bike.

Unity Module

Science laboratory
This is where the astronauts will carry out experiments and astronomical observations.

Escape capsule
This will carry the astronauts back to Earth in an emergency.

Communications antenna
Radio messages are sent to and from the Space Station using dish–like radio aerials or antennas. These antennas are highly directional and can pick up very faint signals.

Zarya Module

USA

BUILDING THE SPACE STATION

The world's most exciting space project, the International Space Station, is currently being built 350 kilometres (217 miles) in orbit above the Earth. Assembly of the Space Station began in December 1998 and will be completed in 2004. The Space Station will be a gigantic 108 metres (354 feet) across and 88 metres (148 feet) long. It will weigh over 430 tonnes (423 tons). It will take 45 shuttle launches to carry the construction parts of the station into orbit.

NASA (National Aeronautics and Space Administration) will carry out most of the construction work and provide most of the modules that make up the station. Russia, Europe, Japan, Canada and Brazil will also take part in the building and operation of the station.

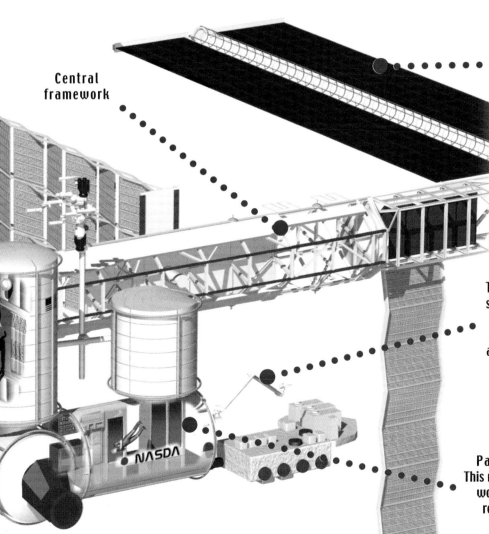

Central framework

Solar panels
These provide the Space Station with power from the Sun. Two huge panels of solar cells, each the size of a football pitch, convert sunlight into electricity.

Robot arm
This is used to grasp and repair satellites. It is controlled by an astronaut inside the Space Station. Video cameras on the arm let the astronaut see what the arm is doing.

Payload servicing module
This module will have a pressurized workshop where the crew will repair and service satellites.

LIVING AND WORKING IN SPACE

The station will have modules for astronauts to live and work in. The modules will be attached to a long spine of inter-connecting beams called a truss. Huge solar panels will supply the station with electricity.

Up to seven astronauts will spend up to three months at a time working in the station. They will carry out all kinds of experiments and observations in orbit. The almost complete absence of gravity on the Space Station will allow experiments that are impossible on Earth. The station will also be used for recovering and repairing weather and communications satellites.

Index